T0128567

The Story Of Two Friends

Ms.Farhat Bakhsh

authorHOUSE®

AuthorHouse™
1663 Liberty Drive
Bloomington, IN 47403
www.authorhouse.com
Phone: 1-800-839-8640

Imagination of an author can sometimes go wide. It is up to the readers to decide to take my story as fiction or non-fiction. Enjoy reading!

First published by AuthorHouse   01/04/2012

ISBN: 978-1-4678-6963-8 (sc)
ISBN: 978-1-4678-6961-4 (ebk)

Library of Congress Control Number: 2011960199

Printed in the United States of America

Any people depicted in stock imagery provided by Thinkstock are models, and such images are being used for illustrative purposes only.
Certain stock imagery © Thinkstock.

This book is printed on acid-free paper.

It all started with a simple hello and ended in a thick friendship where every breath of your friend is counted. Every moment is felt. Every word is cherished and every thought is admired. This is the story of two friends who came together for a certain period of time to be bonded in a lifelong friendship. Yes! The story is about Simran, Raj and Sam.

Simran is a very homely and simple being who tries to experiment her life in a completely different way contrast to what life she has lived till now.

Raj is a mature, handsome and famous guy is surrounded with all sorts of people who carry a false smile all the time is in need of genuine and simple love finds in Simran and gets attracted to her.

Sam is a little young and cute girl, a teenager and very intelligent becomes friendly to Simran on her foreign trip. Something was there in her similar to Raj which attracted Simran.

The two friends Simran and Raj were known to each other before she met Sam. It started with a simple admiration note only to turn into a passion and then care and finally love. Both the friends started interacting with each other. Both of them felt peace in each other's company even though it happened very passively from Raj.

Don't know but something was pushing Simran to the direction of her friend Raj. May be he loved her so much that automatically she is attracted to him or driven in that direction. It is he who loved her first. She starts typing the messages to him and each time the message is selected she is thrilled. Every day is fun only if she is in touch with her friend. She also likes him but respects him more. She gradually starts feeling for him. And she includes him in her prayers he is the first one who gets this privilege. The time passes like that. Meanwhile while interacting she gets her purpose in life. She always wanted to give the message of peace. She gets this opportunity now and she wants to utilise it to the maximum.

She is so happy to pass messages she feels connected. She gets a new Id too. She is now connected to her friend through music. Both the friends share the same passion for music. She enjoys her new self. She wants to have lots of fun and she does. Slowly Slowly she starts caring for him. She tries to find out more about him his likes, dislikes, his hobbies, his past, his friends, his interests everything. She wants to know more and more about him. She starts thinking about him.

She finds out many similarities between her and Raj. And she feels that they share equal interests. She finds their thoughts are matching too. It seems he doesn't mind her taking interest in him. It seems he likes her and finds her interesting. He gives all her comments. She is happy and discovers a new side of hers. She never knew that she also has this sense of humour.

She is changing . . Completely different to what she is! She now wants to be more sportive, she laughs, crack jokes, she pulls his legs through comments, and she really enjoys making him nervous. She takes care of herself now. She wants to look pretty. She feels attracted to him and starts thinking about him as a friend who is there to understand her to what she wants to say and also guide her when she is wrong. She thanks to almighty for giving her such a wonderful friend. She sends him cards, gifts, chocolates and flowers. She loves her friend so much.

She also gets one more way to be in touch with her friend. She joins a social networking site and her friend is happened to be there. It is here on this site she feels so close to her friend. Her life takes a new turn. She defines her goal. She feels like using this medium to help her spread her thoughts. She starts very right and also feels connected to her friend. She is so happy to share her thoughts. She is honest. She shares the story of a young girl and feels her thoughts to be matching of hers. She uses the words of that story to express herself. While sharing her thoughts she feels peaceful, relax and content.

Meanwhile she had to go out of the country on an important visit and may be for a long time. She just can't think of being away from her friend. It is only a matter of 15-20 days or so but she felt missing . . She sends Raj the message and takes leave for not being there. Till this time she didn't know how much she cares for him. Then when she goes abroad all the time she thinks of her friendship. She is amazed she wants to define what was happening to her. Why the thoughts of him with her? She is searching for the answers. Her thoughts are occupied by him. She wants to know what he think of her. She can figure out only this much that he has lot of care for her.

Now she realises when she is away from her friendship that how much she cares! During her stay there she meets a young girl called with love Sam. Both become friendly as if they know each other for long. She spends most of the time with her. In her company she feels she is . . happy! They play all sorts of games shares jokes discuss their likes and dislikes. She feels at ease with her. Most of the time she was with her may be searching for her friend. The time abroad passes quickly in her company. The time comes for her return. She is happy to go back but feels now to be away from Sam. She gives Sam the same Id which Raj gave to her. Thats her favourite ID and maybe she wanted Sam to share it. Also she wanted her to be in touch.

Simran comes back home and happy to interact again with Raj. She couldn't tell him how much she missed him. Life is back to normal for her but she didn't know then a big change was waiting to come in her life. She is very innocent she never think and act very honest. But destiny had some other plans for her. She was going to appear for a biggest test of her life. Everything is going to change for her. Simran as usual busy following her friend and passing messages. She thinks of Sam very often. One day she gets a mail from Sam and she is more than happy. She replies back. Don't know? But there was something regarding those mails she felt she is not receiving from Sam. Sam asked her about her age which she finds very odd. She was worried and doubtful so she tells Raj about this. Sam asks her to come on Chat which she agrees to later. But deep in her heart she was scared to talk to a stranger if that was not Sam. Sam fixes the timing for chat and she replies yes! Both the friends starts chatting . .

First Chat: It is a Friday afternoon. Both friends are ready to talk. Sam sends a confirmation mail for the chat. After wishing each other Sam tells her she is very interesting to that she replies to Sam even Sam is very interesting. But Simran finds it very formal and couldn't imagine Sam to talk so formal with her but then may be distance matters . . Then Sam asks her if she is alone at home to that she replies yes! But for one sec she feels very scared. One thing about Simran she is so engrossed in her friendship with Raj that she feels as if she is talking to him. But when Sam shares with her all the memories of her stay abroad she is confused. Suddenly her mood is off! She gives some excuse to Sam and cut short her chat but tells her to come next day. She is so much confused that why she is feeling so much love for Sam. Not that regular one but something very intense. She doesn't know why she is getting those feelings for that little girl. Something was definitely wrong with her. It was all because of Raj she feels that way but she is happy to talk to Sam because she was taking her there where perhaps she wanted to go . .

Chat II: Both friends meet again. Sam shares some jokes with her and also tells her to find jokes for her. So she does surfing and selects some jokes for her which she shares with her. But Simran is not at ease she only feels like sharing her friendship with her. Sam asks her about her mood to that she replies her mood is not that good when Sam asks why? Simran replies that she is missing her friend. Sam asks her who is her friend to that she says yes someone is there. Then Sam doesn't ask much. But she feels like telling her everything about Raj but then she waits for the next time. She feels Sam is the one with whom she can share her secrets. To change her mood Sam tells her more jokes she laughs her mood is ok to some extent. Sam talks about her school her friends her hobbies her family everything. But Simran was in her own world she listens to Sam but is very eager to tell her everything about Raj. Sam understands her silence and takes a leave.

Chat III: Simran is waiting for Sam to be online. Sam had told her that she can only talk to her in the evening because morning she goes to school. She waits in the evening for Sam. She feels as if Sam knows she is there online but purposely comes late. One more thing about Sam she comes to know she knows computer so well. Sam comes on chat first thing she asks about her mood? To that Simran replies Ok! But now straight way she tells her that she is missing her friend whom she has not yet met. Sam is surprised like anything she asks her how can it be possible if she has not met her friend how can she miss him. Simran tells her that to be true and she tells her she loves her friend so much. Sam shows as if she can't believe all that and she tells her not to talk silly. Sam must be shocked but she doesn't show. She tells her to talk something else. But she keeps on telling her about Raj only. Sam is tired of her talk and disconnect.

Chat IV: Once both the friends talk about their interests their likes and dislikes. They both have love for music. Sam asks Simran what type of music she likes? Simran replies Indian classical music. Then Simran asks Sam which music she prefers so Sam replies she likes western music and songs. Simran teases Sam and calls her an English man. Sam doesn't like it seems so she changes the topic. She asks Simran about books which books she likes so Simran tells her all types of books she reads. Simran asks Sam which books she likes so Sam replies she likes novel. But Sam suggests Simran books like 'twilight' 'moon' and 'eclipse'. May be Sam thought her to be very childish and feels Simran likes only books on the topic of love or she saw Simran discussing mostly love on her social profile. Whatever is the reason but Simran knew now that person not be Sam because Sam won't go for western music being so conservative or she won't read novel being so young. Once again Simran feels she is talking to someone very mature.

Chat V: This is a very passionate chat because first time Simran felt that she is not talking to Sam but somebody else may be Raj. Sam asks her if she can help her in her science project so Simran says why not. Sam tells her to wait so that she can send her the figure. Sam sends the figure via mail and when Simran sees that she is pleasantly surprised! She knew very well and could make out that all the scientific names were pasted on the body of topless male model. That was not the image generally used in science project. It was as if the male model was taken and the labels were pasted on him. First time she feels intimate to Sam but controls herself and reply very normal that just make a chart on the paper or cardboard. She also tells her she could have helped her in completing the project but she is very far from her. To this Sam replies Yes! You are very far you can't help. She understands everything she knows she is not talking to Sam because can't imagine Sam to flirt like this with her. But then who is that person Raj? Don't know why but again and again she feels only Raj can talk like that with her nobody else. She starts feeling love for Raj. She is waiting Sam to come next. She is also a bit scared because Sam being so simple and cute little girl will never send her that image . . And also to think suppose if that person is not Sam somebody else. But then she thinks how come he knows everything about her, her stay abroad, what she did? She thinks Sam shared it with someone? She is totally confused.

Chat VI: One more chat she remembers where she felt so close to Sam. That evening as usual both the friends were talking. Sam talks about her dad and bro. Then suddenly she tells Simran that I am very soft soft and only my dad and bro can touch me and then she tells Simran that only she can't touch her. Now Simran didn't know what to reply she was all loss of words . . She felt so much for Sam that day. Because she already knew Sam was not fat Sam was ditto like

Simran thin and delicate. Now all the more Simran thinks there is someone other than Sam she was talking to. And she can't imagine that person to be other than Raj. She controls herself once again and tells Sam yeah! She knows she can't touch her. But at that moment she feels like running to that direction where Sam is and simply hug her friend tight and don't leave. She feels so much of love!

Special Chat: It was a cosy evening Sam was in a very good mood. She tells Simran to play eye-eye game. This game they used to play very often when they met abroad and really used to enjoy it. Always Simran used to win and Sam used to feel so upset. Except once or twice when Sam won she was very happy. Sam's eyes were so big and beautiful and Simran loved to just stare in those innocent eyes for a long time so not to blink. And Sam couldn't bear those sharp stare used to blink very often. That day when Sam tells her to play eye game Simran recalls all those moments which she had spent with her and was so much of fun. But now to play that game she felt so shy to think Raj is there on other side and teasing her. She agrees to Sam even though she couldn't see Sam, her beautiful eyes just peeped in front of her. Simran smiles she tries to concentrate. But thinking of Raj she feels so shy that automatically she looks down and her eyes blink. She tells Sam you win but Sam might have felt that way too so she says you win. That day first time Simran felt Raj's presence and she couldn't help but to be quiet and surrender.

ChatVII: In the beginning Simran finds Sam very honest to her and when Sam shares with her all the details she really feels wanted. One thing she likes about Sam that sometimes she talked so mature but then she just can't believe it to be Sam. One such occasion was when Sam informs her that there is a function in her dad's office next Sunday so she won't be there. She has to go out of town. Suddenly Simran feels very important also she feels that person to be Raj because no one can share the details with so much of fineness with her. And to imagine it to be Sam looked hardly possible. This Sam tells her in One week advance and that only Raj could do because he could only plan his schedules in advance she thinks like that. Any ways she feels very happy and proud of her friendship. She loved Sam more that day imagining her to be her Raj. One more important thing which forces Simran to think Sam is Raj that she had command over language and that perfectness was not possible for a sixth std girl. And also Simran had talked with her so much so she knew her fluency in English language. Simran was never careful about spellings during chat but Sam used to get really annoyed if she did any spelling error . . She used to actually shout at Simran and Simran used to feel so awkward and found Sam sound just like an editor of a news paper.

ChatVIII: Sam never took her name Simran finds this very odd. She thinks this can happen only if that person feels so close to her and feels love for her and to hide that love doesn't want to take her name. But then there was no need for Sam to think like that she had all the freedom to call her in whatever way she wants. Simran is forced to think she is talking to someone who is not comfortable in taking her name. So she asks Sam if she knows her name to that Sam replies yes and calls her by the name. Now Simran is really confused she feels may be Sam doesn't like her name so she asks Sam to give her a new name. Sam may be surprised she doesn't understand to why Simran is asking her about a new name. One more reason to why Simran forces Sam to suggest her some other name because she wanted that name to be only for her friend no one else to share that name. She wants only Sam to call her by that name and that will be very special to her. Why only name whatever her friend tells her she finds it very special and close to her heart. Yeah! So Sam sends her a list of few names via mail which she sees afterwards and becomes so happy because that list includes a name which was her favourite. Sam also suggests her favourite name. She replies to Sam and calls her darling for including her favourite name in the list. She also forces Sam to call her with this new name. Simran is more than happy to get the new name.

Chat IX: Simran is desperate to tell Sam everything about Raj. How she feels? What madness she did? What she thinks? Everything. So that day she tells Sam that she wants to tell her about her friend. Then she says she has written actually counts & tells so many messages for Raj. How she is following him like a mad. She also tells Sam how much she has cried for Raj. Also how much time she thinks about him and how many messages she sent to him. While telling all this she actually cries and tells Sam may be after all this Raj doesn't care for her. Sam first time sends her a kiss. She feels good! Relaxed to share with Sam her personal feelings. But then she feels bad to think what that little young girl must be thinking about her. And to her fear Sam doesn't come for chat for two three days. She waits for Sam to come online. When Sam comes next she tells Simran she has written a poem on school and study. So Simran tells her she would like to read. Sam sends her the poem via mail. That poem was written just like without head or tail but then from VIth Std student what you expect. Simran reads it but doesn't know how to react when Sam asks her whether she liked the poem Simran replies yes! Nice it is. Sam expects her to tell more but Simran was not in a position to add anything. She feels as if Sam was teasing her by writing purposely such poem which hardly carried weight or may be that was the one more way of showing she is Sam only and nobody else. Sometimes Sam really talked foolish and sometimes very intelligent. Simran was damn confused to such kind of behaviour. Sometimes Simran is so scared and also feels upset for her helplessness that she can't reach to Sam.

Chat X: Next day again both the friends were just chatting. Sam tells her about her school. Then she tells her my best

13

friend has ditched me so Simran asks her why what happened? So Sam tells her that she became friendly to some other friend and not talking to her. Simran tells her then you talk to her. She also tells her whoever loves more has to compromise. But Sam was in a different mood she kept on repeating the same thing and Simran was explaining her in different ways. Simran couldn't understand to what she meant. At that time she couldn't figure out that was meant for her. Sam doesn't come on chat for one two days Simran can't figure out what wrong? Then when Sam comes next she sends her one song which meant I tried to forget you but your thoughts made me cry. Now something clicks to Simran she thinks she shared with her love for Raj so she felt bad or she feels may be Sam is Raj and is hurt when she talked with him about her friendship. Simran had till then not shared the name of her friend. So she decides to share next time the Raj's name with Sam. She tells Sam to send her poems which Sam sends her. She likes those poems so much that she gives a very lovable name to Sam. And Sam also likes that name.

Chat XI: Simran is worried now for her friendship. She feels she did something wrong by sharing her secrets with Sam what she must be thinking about her but she can't help it. She feels very close to Sam. She trusts her and also Sam was helping her indirectly to cope up with all the emotional tides she was facing at that time. Now she wanted Sam all the more. One day she doesn't talk to her she feels uneasy. Unknowingly

Sam had become the part of her life. Also because she had equated in mind Sam to be her Raj. And then one day again Simran felt confident of her thoughts. That evening Sam was in a good mood. She talks to Simran very nicely. Then she asks Simran to imagine both of them meet each other. Simran says ok! Then Sam asks her to introduce herself. She tells the name which Sam like. Then she asks Sam whats her name then you know what Sam replies? "Marry Me!" Simran is mum she looks again at the spellings and is sure that can't be the spelling error from her English Scholar friend he meant marry only and not Mary. She controls her feelings and says "nice name!" Sam thinks she didn't get it and may be upset so cut short the chat. Simran is just lost . . She doesn't know what was happening to her at that moment she knew now the person she is talking to is not little Sam. He actually popped up the big question and proposed her & she prays in her heart that person to be Raj.

Chat XII: Now again Sam talks about her school she might be worried if Simran got a doubt. Simran also talks quite normal so not to show that she knows now he can't be Sam. Sometimes Sam talked very childish and sometimes very mature. Simran is bound to think whether she talked to two persons she thinks may be Raj also talks to her along with Sam. She just can't make out. Sam sometimes says she has a friend in the same town where Raj lived so she thinks may be Sam and Raj know each other and helping each other to talk to her. Nothing she can tell with surety because she herself wanted to know all the answers and she knew only one person can reply to all her questions and that is Sam. So she waits for the right time to ask Sam about everything that disturbed her mind.

Sam rarely talked to Simran on Saturdays and Sundays. So Sat and Sun she feels so sad! She waits for Sam in front of her computer by chance if she comes. But Sam was not there. Simran thinks if Sam goes to school then on Sat Sun she gets holiday and on these days she should be more free to talk to her. But it was opposite. Then she thinks Sam must be Raj because Sat Sun is off to him and he must be busy doing other work or simply relax at home and not to think of office and her. On these days she feels so sad and misses Sam all the more. She realizes she is in complete love with Raj. Now she can actually feel the pain inside her heart. She also tries to keep herself busy but she finds out she is completely taken over by the thoughts of Raj. Wherever she goes whatever she does her mind is all filled up with only one thought and that is of Raj. So most of the time she is only physically present to where she is! She waits curiously for Monday so that she will be back with Sam. A big change is slowly emerging in Simran's life. She is getting detached to everything around. Yes! She is moving to some other world where at the end of the day she remains completely isolated. Yes! Her feelings for her friend is more intense more subtle and more loved.

Chat XII: That evening Sam again asks her age so Simran is nervous again. Sam tells her she wants to open her facebook account. Simran from first is not that comfortable with facebook so she refuses Sam. To that Sam asks her why she is scared or what? To that Simran replies no! But she is not in favour of opening an account on facebook and she reminds her that she has already told her when they met and were talking abroad. But Sam didn't want to hear anything. She tells her she has done so much for her on facebook . . To this Simran wonders what she has done for her. Reply to this she finds out later. When Sam again forces her Simran tells her put any age the same reply which she gave to Sam when she had asked her to add her to contacts on her favourite ID. But now she was thinking when how or if Sam too have opened an account or she already had then why she didn't tell her earlier. But then she had thought its Raj's ID too and perhaps he wanted to add her to quick contacts out of his unlimited list.

Sam goes ahead and opens her facebook account and tells her to log in. She tries to log in but she couldn't. She tells Sam she can't log in till then she didn't know much about computer. Sam is the one who teaches her all the functions of chat and networking. Sam doesn't believe it and tells her she is telling lie. Anyways Sam tries to help her to log in but she could not do it so she tells her to end for the day. Simran is just sitting on the desk and thinking whether to move forward or not. Now she is worried and thinks if Sam is not Raj or somebody else what Raj will think about her all wrong. She didn't want this so she sends a mail to Sam telling her she only love Raj and he is only important to her and she can't imagine to talk to anybody else. She feels bad to think how Sam has forcibly opened her account first time was not showing respect to her feelings. Sam neither replies to her mail nor comes on chat. Now Simran starts feeling so sad she cries and cries. She just can't imagine being away from Sam. So she gives up and she didn't know that time this is the biggest mistake she is going to do of her life to compromise with wrong. But then she feels she can do that much for her little friend whom she loves so much and also in some corner of her heart she had a hope of Sam to be her Raj. Yes! She was taking risk. Perhaps a biggest risk in her friendship. She sends Sam e-mail to be on facebook in the evening saying she is ready to be there. And she tells the world that if you do something what your friend wants you to do is worth doing . .

Special chat: One thing both the friends realise they love each other very much. Its not just the exchange of words its exchange of thoughts and love too. Many a times they just be there and don't speak any word. As if they wanted that silence to be there so that they get some time to feel each other. Yes! Simran felt that very much. She loved that silence she loved that bond between her and her friend. She didn't want those moments to end . . She starts feeling strongly for her friend and she is sure what she is feeling is possible only with Raj not with Sam. So compatible she felt! Now it was not possible for her to imagine for a second to be away from her friend.

Chatfb1: A new world completely different for Simran she was not comfortable to . . First thing she does she checks whether Raj is there or not and when she finds Raj she is more than happy what more she wanted. She puts Raj's name in her list of friends till then she didn't know the difference between page and people and she had put Raj's page in the list. But she was happy then. She sees Sam's profile also. Her friends what games she prefers her school her interest everything. Now she knew she was talking to Sam only. She feels dejected . . But why Sam had to show all her details to her so that she will believe her to be Sam and no one else. Later when she recalls her talk before opening facebook account that she has done so much for her here she realises that account was specifically opened for her to believe she was talking to Sam only and no one else. But that was hard for her to believe at any point through all her talking to Sam you know why? because she loved Raj truly and heart can never tell lie when in true love. But the truth she was eager to know only from Raj and she had the hope that one day her friend will speak truth.

On here on facebook she finds Sam completely different to what she was before. She couldn't believe is this Sam or someone else. Sam tells her she is a facebook freak. She also sees on facebook two Ids with the same name it means all these days or on facebook she talked to two persons may be? She doesn't know. But who is this other person she is curious to know . .

Chartfb2: Sam comes on chat talks all love with her. Sam is there on Sunday she can't believe! Sam tells her to play games with her now Simran finds it very odd all of a sudden such a change! She tries to play but she couldn't. She finds it very childish so she stops. She gives some excuse to Sam and tells her she doesn't want to waste time in games she just want to talk to her. Sam feels bad may be. Simran decides to share Raj's name with her thinking if Sam is Raj he must know who is her friend so won't misunderstand her. So Simran asks Sam "you know who is my friend?" to that Sam replies, "No!" So Simran tells her that her friends name is Raj and if she knows him? because Raj is so famous. Sam replies yes! She knows him. Simran is happy to hear that she asks Sam "How is he?" to that Sam replies "I don't know". Simran wanted to hear something from her for Raj so she again repeats her question. Sam replies same but in a happy tone so Simran feels ok. She feels if Sam is Raj then hopefully his doubt is cleared. She is relaxed now to share the name with Sam. She hopes Sam to be Ok now like her very own. But don't know why Sam continues to behave odd with her on facebook. She was not same any more . .

Chatfb3: She talks all silly first time Simran feels a change in Sam's talk. She is all so upset that is she never wanted and really feels very sad . . Sam gives her names she is shocked she could never believe Sam can talk like that also with her. Sam was talking mannerless with her. She couldn't bear that. She feels may be she talked with her about Raj so Sam felt bad and no more gives respect to her. So Simran tells sorry to her and says she won't talk like that in future and she knows she did mistake. But Sam was not talking like before. Simran feels NO! that can't be Sam that cute little girl she knows and also she now can't think that person to be Raj because that much sure she was that Raj respects her and he is such a person that he won't hurt anyone leave alone Simran. Then who is that person she was talking to? She is worried! One more thing Sam asked her once she doesn't get scared or what? Simran thinks for a moment why Sam is asking this question to her what is the purpose of this question. Then she replies to Sam she is born brave and that is the fact what she told. Simran is that type she always speaks the truth and she knows when you speak truth you don't have to get scared of anyone. She doesn't hide anything. May be Sam didn't know this or perhaps Simran didn't feel the need to tell her that her people at home knows everything about her friendship. They know how much she cares for Raj. They also know what she is going through. Simran has already described her feelings to them. But how could she explain this to a VIth std girl and why she thinks so.

Now when Sam goes on talking like that she feels very bad. First time they both fight with each other. Simran also tells Sam so much she actually shouts at her for talking senseless! Sam also tells her whatever she wants. Simran asks her she can't be her Sam so Sam asks her who is she? Simran doesn't reply to that question she is so angry she just wanted to know who is that person she is talking to? and what the truth is! But then again Sam changes realising her mistake and what she asked to Simran so replies very coolly she is only Sam but Simran didn't want to believe it ever. She tells Sam to come on chat on her old Id facebook is not good for them they are fighting there and she doesn't like to fight with her. But Sam doesn't listen to her she tells her she likes facebook very much. Simran had to give up! She wants now Sam to be there.

Chatfb4: It was Sunday morning. Simran checks Sam is there on facebook she is surprised again otherwise Sam never came on Sat Sun to chat. She asks Simran what she is doing? Simran tells her she is doing all household work cleaning cooking washing taking study and talking to her. Then Simran asks Sam what are you doing? Sam tells her she is playing games. Simran asks her what are her interests other than games? At the same time she is worried now Sam will ask her to play games because she doesn't have that much patience to do that. Sam replies she plays games and do cooking and so much of work. Now it was hard for Simran to digest how can it be her Mom she knew won't allow her to cook and work all the time so surprised she is so she asks Sam it can't be but Sam tells her that is only the fact. Simran asks Sam if she can call her Raj so Sam agrees to her. Simran is so happy because first time she felt Sam agreed to be Raj. Simran tells her thank you at least she accepted his name. Sam doesn't say anything But Simran is relaxed first time she felt she found her Raj. That day she really felt close to him.

Special chat: Yes! Cooking reminds Simran of something very lovable what happened that evening. She was as usual busy thinking of Raj and was looking at his photograph and she missed him so badly that she switched on the computer with a hope if Sam is there. She just acts as if she is checking the mail suddenly Sam comes for chat she is sooooooo happy in her heart she wanted that only but she doesn't tell Sam about it. Instead she asks Sam what she is doing there? And if she doesn't have any work or what? Sam doesn't reply to that and asks her what she is doing so Simran tells her she is just checking her mail. Then Simran asks Sam to go to that Sam tells she won't. Simran doesn't like to go before Sam. She tells her to go but Sam tells no and asks her not to go. Simran tells Sam now she has to cook and she can't continue. Even though that day Simran felt very strongly for Raj she felt so much of love for him and she knew she is talking to Raj only she had to discontinue because at that time she had not told anyone about her friendship at home and they were about to come. So Simran takes a leave.

Fb Chat5: Simran tries to adjust herself on the facebook. She does whatever Sam tells her to do. Now Sam knows her weakness so she tries to take her for granted. She doesn't talk to her properly. She comes at any time and goes at any time. She doesn't care for Simran more. She back replies her or talks all vague with her. Sam just waits for an excuse to fight with Simran and Simran couldn't make out to what is happened to Sam and why she is behaving this way with her. Sam again talks in such a manner that Simran gets very angry and she decides to deactivate her facebook account. One two days both of them don't talk but then Sam comes on her old Id to chat. Its very difficult for Simran to get angry on Sam for long so she also starts talking to her.

Then Sam again activates her Facebook account and tells Simran to turn a new leaf. Both the friends again start chatting and everything looks back to normal. But then Simran does some craziest things. In order to just make Sam happy she clicks her photograph in modern clothes pants and shirt and coat. She looked completely contrast to what she is. And she sends that photograph via FB message for Sam. But when Sam sees those photographs she gets very angry and tells her she doesn't know who she is and goes away. Simran is so upset she had thought she would make Sam happy and she never thought that Sam will get so much annoyed. Sam doesn't talk to her for one week or so Simran sends her so many messages then finally she remembers that topless model photo which Sam had sent her so she reminds Sam about that. Then may be Sam understood that she got it what she sent to her. And Simran also tells her that she just clicked those photographs at home only and she didn't go anywhere in that dress. Now Sam was fine and she came on chat. But Simran kept on thinking why her dressing created so much of tension for Sam who is so young to think like that. She just can't believe she knows there is definitely someone quite elder who didn't like her wearing that dress but then who is that person if not Sam she is worried.

Chatfb6 : That day as usual Sam was not in a correct mood. She says hi to Simran and then starts talking all so different. She tells Simran now she can't be there on facebook even though she likes facebook so much. This is what worried Simran so she asks her what is the reason she had told her that on facebook she will be there all the time and Simran remembers she was so happy. Then suddenly what happened that she is no more interested in being there. Simran feels very Sad! She wanted her Sam back. But Sam doesn't reply properly. It seems she doesn't find Simran worth to share more. Simran is hurt! She understood everything the purpose of Sam in opening her facebook account. So she asks Sam only to track her movements she did open her account? Sam doesn't reply. So Simran thinks that to be the only reason behind opening her account on facebook Sam must be wanting to find out everything about her . . her contacts her friends the sites she visits what she does? But then Simran doesn't have anything to hide. She is so open. One secret to share from the beginning Simran knows Sam is there and watches her and she doesn't mind actually. She loves her friend so much.

Chatfb7: That day they fought like anything. The topic was such that made Simran all wild. Sam talked about her country. She was telling something which Simran didn't want to hear. For time being Simran forgot everything her friendship that love disappeared. She warned Sam to talk something else but Sam kept on saying all the things which made Simran more angry and she again warned Sam to not bring her country in between their friendship. But where Sam was listening she continued her talk now Simran was furious. She could not take that any longer she burst on Sam. That day really she shouted at Sam like anything. She cries like anything because she knew now everything is over between both the friends. Simran decides to deactivate her account once more. May be Sam felt she is wrong. She tells Simran they will talk on her old ID but Simran says no! At that moment she just wanted to go from there. She was hurt once again and this time very badly. She could never compromise on her principles and Sam was asking something similar to that.

Chat1: Simran was at herself that evening and was thinking of her friendship. Sam comes on chat. Simran couldn't resist she talks to Sam. She tells her that facebook was not lucky for them. They just fought there. Then Sam replies sometimes if I want we can chat on facebook. Now Simran is annoyed she tells Sam not to talk like a street Romeo. So may be Sam feels bad she is quiet. Both the friends again start chatting. Its same like before but something is missing Simran feels like that. Now Sam comes very rarely to chat. Simran sends her messages. She gives excuses of her school and homework. Simran waits for her online whole day but Sam doesn't come. One thing Simran felt that Raj is definitely there and watching all the pain she is going through. Even if she didn't talk to Raj he saw and heard everything. And for Simran that was enough to live!

Chat2: One day both the friends were talking. Now Simran takes care that she doesn't say anything wrong to her friend. She wants to give some gift to Sam. So she asks Sam that she wants to send her some gifts but Sam tells her she doesn't want anything. She also asks Simran how will she send that gift by post or what? Simran tells her to leave that to her and she is expert in sending gifts she will either send it by post or courier. Then Sam didn't know what to reply so she says she doesn't want anything. Simran is upset she tells Sam you don't send any thing to me but let me send you some gift. Sam is quiet and doesn't reply then Simran asks her if she will call her. To that Sam doesn't reply and just goes offline . . Simran is so confused she thinks if she is her Sam then what is the problem in calling her or giving her the gift. She feels sad to think how long to wait to meet her friend. Day by day Simran becomes more desperate to meet Sam.

Facebook : One day Simran was just thinking of Sam and so she remembers facebook she reactivates her facebook account with a hope Sam will be there. But Sam doesn't come for chat. So she just goes through Pages of Raj. She types Raj so she comes to know there are people with that name. That day she finds out that Raj's one more account is there and that is actually his account and all these days she was looking was only a page. She is happy for her discovery at the same time she thinks she is such a dumb didn't know the difference between page and people. Anyway she starts going through the list of Raj's friends and family. She finds out something hidden and pleasing to her about Raj's family that she is surprised. In her madness she sends a friend request to his family. And thats it! that was a mistake she wished she had not done. She is so innocent that she tells Raj that she was so happy to know more about his family and feels connected. She waits for one two days more on facebook. Then that day Sam sends her a message that she is withdrawing from facebook. She won't be there. She removes her account. Simran couldn't send her the message or find her account. Simran feels so uneasy. One thing about facebook whenever Simran tries to go away from it she feels so much pain and also she feels she is going away from someone who belongs to her. Thats why always she cries so much whenever she deactivates her account.

Fb Special: That day as usual Simran was going through all the pages and people of facebook. She misses Sam so much! So she tries to send message to her. But she couldn't. She tries other options which facebook suggests. Like sending messages through email Id. So she tries typing Sam's Id. Facebook asks for birth date. She knew Raj's date of birth so she types that and to her pleasant surprise she could access Sam's Id and could send the message to Sam. Simran is so overwhelmed she knows now and she knew before Sam is only Raj. She is relaxed she is happy what more she wanted. Later when Sam came on her ID to chat she kept asking Simran how she found out her secret and Simran pretended thinking Sam to be Raj that what she is talking about. Deep in her heart she knew Sam was talking about how she was successful in finding out the secret of Raj's ID.

Tough chat: Once more Sam comes online to chat on facebook but she chats via messages. Simran had by mistake in anger deleted Sam's name from friends list so the list of Raj also disappears. Simran thinks Sam is only Raj and he only had attached his page to Sam's account . . That day Sam talked to her via messages only Simran was begging her to put Raj's name again in the list but she kept asking" why did you delete my name?" Simran her not to feel bad tells her that happened by mistake. Then Sam asks for the password to do that so Simran gives her the password which she had given to her and Simran had again changed just before that. That password was given to her by Sam but while deactivating her account Simran had changed that password fearing Sam to change that and she won't be able to access her account then. May be her trust for Sam had fallen at that time. That was a beautiful password given to her by Sam 'hidden beauty' and Simran really liked it. But then what that password meant again forced Simran to think that person not to be Sam because she was known to Sam. Sam realised or had found out that the password is changed so she tells Simran may be she thought Simran had changed the password. Simran remains quiet. That day Sam just talked anything as if something was troubling her. And so Simran feels purposely Sam was talking all vague and Sam knew it was hurting Simran. May be Sam had felt very bad to know Simran had deleted her name.

When Sam doesn't add the name and Simran asks her again and again she asks her "what to do give my life?" Before also and now whenever Sam spoke like that talking to give her life Simran felt very bad she feels as if she can't breathe don't know why but whenever Sam spoke like that it was very hurting for Simran. She felt so much pain. She somehow thinks her Raj is talking like that and to think that way she feels as if she too can't breathe. Simran wants Raj to be always happy and whenever Sam talked like that she felt Raj is upset and she just can't bear that feeling. For one hour or so she just talked with Simran anything which really had no meaning. Simran was tired first time she felt exhausted to talk to Sam. It never happened before. Finally Sam adds Raj's name to the list and asks Simran if she is happy. To that Simran replies yes! But what Simran missed to note that Sam had not put her name back in the list . .

Chat3 : Now Sam came very rarely to talk to Simran as if slowly slowly her friend is getting bored! Simran waits hours for her friend to come online and when she comes she hardly talks and goes away. Simran feels very bad she couldn't do anything. Only on one click Sam used to disappear. Simran doesn't mind because she is the only one who is her friend to share everything about Raj. She doesn't want to lose Sam so she tolerates all the anger and wrong behaviour of Sam for the sake of Raj. Now Sam gets angry on her very often. Simran doesn't say a word. More she talks to Sam more she loves Raj. Her feeling of friendship and care gives way to true love she feels for him. She is in touch with Raj through messages. She desperately wants Raj now to be her friend. Meanwhile Sam starts ignoring her. With so much of love facebook account was opened for her now deserted. Whenever Simran tries to close her facebook profile she gets a feeling as if she is going far from someone very close she feels very low and starts crying if she attempts to do that. So she asks Sam to close her account thinking Sam will never do that but one day to her surprise Sam closes her account. Simran feels very bad she asks Sam how dare she closed the account and she won't forgive her. But Sam replies very casually that she had only told her. Simran is so confused to why Sam had first of all opened her account if she didn't want to be there. She had thought Sam has opened that account out of love. Life goes on for Simran. Now most of the time Sam is not there and Simran waits for her like a crazy person. And whenever she comes she mostly fights with her very rarely now they talk of love and friendship.

Chat 4 : Sam tells her she is busy in sports in her school so will get hardly any time for chat. But Simran requests her to be there for some time she can't think of being away from Sam. She is now completely dissolved in her friendship and doesn't want to come out of it. Coincidently Raj too is busy with sports and so Simran once again thinks Sam to be Raj. Once Sam came for chat she was in a very happy mood she tells Simran they won a prize in her school tournament and she tells her she will send her the photograph. Finally! Simran thinks now the suspense will end when Sam will send the photograph she will know She spoke to Sam only all these days. So she tells Sam she will be happy to see her at last! But again when Sam sends her the photograph she sends only of the medal which was nicely kept on a sheet. But there was no Sam now Simran is so upset she tries to search if that medal photograph is available on her school site and Raj just copied it but she doesn't find it. She but comes to know that there was a tournament in her school. Once again Simran feels sad. And she is thinking why Sam is not sending her photograph to her if she is only Sam.

Chat5: Once both the friends were talking Sam was in a different mood. Now mostly Sam is in such a mood. She asks Simran if she believes in ghosts so Simran replies yes! she does. Then Sam tells her they have a house which is haunted and now her dad would sell it. But that was bought for her and she doesn't want it to be sold. Then she goes on describing how the ghost used to trouble her and she used to be so terrified. Simran tells her not to get scared of ghosts and to feel mercy for them and to pray for them they need that. But Sam goes on talking with her about ghosts it seems she wanted Simran to get scared. But Simran was not! So Sam feels bad. Sam also tells her that that house was bought for her so to give in dowry. Now Simran assuming her to be Raj tells her that don't sell it in future you might need that house to live with someone you love. Sam understands what Simran meant to say and thats why Simran liked her and so she asks Simran will she stay there with her friend? Simran wanted this only to come from Sam she says wholeheartedly Yes! She loves her friend so much that she is ready to live with him anywhere. Now Sam didn't know what to say so she again talks all about selling of house. Then Simran feels Sam is feeling so bad so she tells her if she can buy that for her but then Sam replies at once no no it is sold off. And also Sam tells her specifically they live in a bungalow now! Simran feels bad because she knows Sam won't talk like that with her even though she too stays in a bungalow. Now Simran thinks who is that person showing off!? Simran is such a simple soul that she never believed in wealth and money only thing she craves is a true love!

Special Chat: This is again a chat which assured Simran to feel she is talking to Raj. That day Sam was in a good mood. She did talk to her nicely. Simran was happy she felt her Raj to be so close to her. So she asks Sam if they can meet. To that Sam replies that is not possible here they can only meet in heaven. May be Sam meant to say about the song she sent to her but then Simran felt very sad thinking its not possible to meet her friend or what? She tells Sam yes! She knows they can only meet in heaven and there she won't allow her to go away from her eyes even for a second. She finds Sam more patient and mature in front of her. As if Sam is elder to Simran and always talked like that reminding Simran very often not to talk like a child. Simran loved it when Sam got angry on her and referred her to be a child. She simply enjoyed those moments and didn't want them to end. Whenever she talked about Raj Sam shouted at her and told her not to talk silly. Simran loved those innocent shouting and continued to talk silly. Simran is happy to have Sam in her life.

Simran recalls how much she has completely taken over by her friendship that she doesn't have any control on herself. She can't imagine now to be out of touch with her friend. Once someone at home purposely hid the modem wire so she won't talk. Nobody was there at home. She searches in the whole room for wire but she doesn't find. She just didn't know what to do. She thought of buying a new one. She couldn't wait for some time she couldn't. So she goes to the market. She searches in the whole market for that wire like a mad. She any how wanted it at that moment so to feel she is in touch with her friend. Simran tries to control herself but in vain she then searches more and she gets one then when the system is on she feel relaxed. Even though Sam was not there because it was a morning time she feels peaceful in front of the computer. Don't know what was happening to Simran. She couldn't define her feelings only thing she knew if she goes against it she feels painful. Such was the love for her friend that for that moment she forgot the whole world for Simran her friend is only her world.

Special Chat : That day it was different because Sam promised her to come in the morning. Simran was more than happy she always wanted Sam to come in the morning to chat. But whenever she asked Sam about it Sam replied so harshly saying who will go to school? And she told her strictly that she can only talk to her in the evening. She is allowed to chat only one hour in the evening. Simran gets scared whenever Sam talked like that. She doesn't want her friend to get angry. So Simran doesn't again dare to ask her to come in the morning. But Sam tells her that day tomorrow she has holiday so she can come. Simran tells her jokingly she knows she won't get up so early but deep in her heart she was waiting impatiently for morning to come. That was a lovely morning and Simran was all set to talk to her friend. She knew it is going to be special. Also that morning was very special to remember because that had brought the change Simran was waiting for and praying in a country she also loved. Simran checks in first thing she sees whether Sam is there but Sam was not there. Simran a bit nervous put on the chat and types that she knew Sam will be sleeping and sends and waits and to her pleasant surprise Sam comes online and says she is awake now Simran feels sooooooo happy she wanted this moment to be there for long and that day she was very happy. She asks Sam to ask whatever she wants she will give, thinking Sam to be Raj but Sam tells her she doesn't want anything she has everything. Now Simran feels bad also Sam was talking like a very mature person. What Simran had thought Sam will talk of love which she was feeling very badly that day. But No! Then Simran tells Sam you don't give me anything but tell me what you want. So Sam thinks she felt bad so she says its not like she doesn't want anything from her she wants her wishes to that Simran tells her wishes are always with her. That day Simran really thought she talked with Raj because not possible only for Sam to talk like this so mature and in this way. Sam would have definitely asked for something even very small because she was too young to think so big. Simran felt so much love for Raj that day. And she wanted her friend to ask her to give all her love. And she really wanted to tell him that.

Chat 6: That was a beautiful evening something different. Sam came on the line for chat. She was in a weary mood. She tells Simran one two dirty jokes not vulgar actually but without any sense. Simran feels bore she tells Sam to talk something else but Sam was in a different mood. Sam says No! And sends her more such jokes. Simran feels bore but acts as if she liked those jokes. Then Simran too thinks to send her a forwarded joke which was lying in her mail box. And was similar to those jokes. She asks Sam if she can send her a dirty joke because she was scared if really she happened to be Sam then she will never like it. She asks Sam her Mom won't scold her na? To that Sam says no! She won't. Then Simran sends her that joke by e-mail. She asks Sam if she liked that joke Sam says yes! And then for sometime doesn't say anything. Sam did that many of the time and Simran used to get scared if she remained quiet for a long time.

So Simran thinking she must have felt bad for that dirty joke tells her that it must have been sent by her friend by mistake and so not to think wrong. Then Sam asks her to send her more jokes like that. Now Simran is more scared she couldn't figure out what Sam is exactly up to. So she tries to convince her that really she doesn't know more such jokes and that was the only joke sent to her by her friend so not to misunderstand her. But Sam was in a different mood that day she goes on repeating the same thing. Then Simran remembers long back when she was searching joke for Sam she had read one dirty joke and had simply saved it to laugh if she feels like. She tells Sam this and tells her to hold on so that she will see if it is there. Simran starts searching but it was not there she might have deleted that thinking it to be wrong. She tells Sam its not there but Sam is not ready to listen then what she says surprises Simran like anything and there was a mischievous spark in Simran's eyes for turning her doubt to reality. Sam tells her you are done with it or satisfied what about me I am not. Simran pretends as if she didn't get what Sam was telling she tells Sam really she didn't find it in her documents but promises her to again search on the web. Sam goes offline by repeating the same lines. Simran was worried now she starts searching the web and luckily finds that joke. She immediately sends the joke to Sam and tells her to come online but Sam doesn't. Now it was confirmed to Simran that she was not talking to Sam. The person she was talking to has to be him and not her. Simran can't think Sam to talk like that. And Simran really prayed that person to be Raj because she can't think even in her dream to talk so freely to a stranger.

Chat7: Simran was forcing Sam to come on chat on 14th feb so that she won't miss Raj. But Sam tells her it is not possible she is very busy. One thing Simran felt a difference in Sam that now Sam always tells her she is so busy and so much of work but Simran wonders how come being so little she is so busy and talks about so much of work Simran just can't believe it she feels Sam is Raj and Raj is always busy but natural. Whenever Simran feels this way she feels peace. Then Simran requests Sam more and tells her to come at least for some time. Sam doesn't reply properly but deep in her heart Simran knew Sam will come for chat. On 14th feb Simran waits for Sam the whole evening she was sure Sam will come. And yes to her pleasant surprise Sam comes on chat. But immediately after coming Sam says she is come only for a short time and is very busy. Simran thanks Sam for coming and asks Sam how is she? Sam says fine. Then Simran asks Sam will she come with her to an island. Now Sam shouts at her and Simran really loves her shouting and Sam also tells her not to talk silly. So Simran asks her how was her day Sam tells it to be fine. Then Sam goes away. Simran is so happy with a thought that Raj had come for her specially and Simran felt it to be like that. She knew it before if Sam is Raj then he would definitely come on Valentine's day. And Raj had surely come even if it was for a couple of moments she felt blessed! Simran had also sent flowers to Raj with all the love with a hope of being in touch really. She always felt to give all the nice things as gifts and she feels so much pleasure in doing that. For Raj maybe it was very normal to get gifts being so famous but for Simran it did mean a lot. She gives so much value to him and her friendship. She wants her friend to be always happy.

Chat 8: One more occasion when Simran felt that really she was talking to somebody other than Sam. Women's day approaching and Simran had decided to write some article on men. She purposely asks Sam is it ok if she writes on Men? Sam wholeheartedly says yes! Simran was waiting for that reply. Otherwise all these days Simran had noticed Sam's behaviour to be more conservative and suddenly Sam agreeing to Simran writing on men puts Simran back in her thoughts. So to confirm her belief Simran asks Sam again what everyone will think about her. If they think all wrong then? Sam replies her not to worry about others. This is what Sam wants and it is up to her to decide. Simran was all happy in her heart again tells Sam ok she will write but she will send Sam first what she has written and Sam has to approve it. Sam agrees to that. So Simran writes a positive article on men defending them and she sends Sam that article by e-mail and asks how it is and if it needs any change? Sam comes online and sounds happy and tells Simran her article is ok and no need of any change. Simran feels so happy to get all the praise from Sam and also because she knew now the person she is talking to is a man! **Raj**.

Chat 9: Very special chat for Simran but that day she didn't know this is perhaps the last chat between her and her dear friend. Simran tells Sam to imagine her to be Raj. Sam agrees to that. Then Simran tells Sam to think they are meeting at a book release function where Raj is a chief guest. Simran tells her that she is also there and after the function Simran asks Raj to give her the autograph. Simran had written in that autograph book if he will meet her in the cafe there she wants to have a word with him. Raj writes in that book yes! All this Simran tells Sam to act and really Sam acts so perfectly. Then they meet in the cafe Simran tells Sam to ask her why she wanted to meet him. So Sam asks the same question. Simran replies just like that. Simran orders juice for them. Simran tells Raj she is his biggest fan so she wanted to meet him. Then Simran looks into his eyes and both are silent they don't speak any word and they both feel each other. Then Sam asks Simran what next so Simran tells her to ask her if he can drop her home in his car. Simran agrees to that. Sam asks her if she sits in front so Simran replies no! She sits in the back seat. Then Raj asks her where she stays? to that Simran wanted to say she stays in his heart but controls herself and says Nepean Sea Road. Then both become quiet as if feeling the moment which was full of love. Sam acts so perfectly that not for a single sec Simran felt she is not Raj. Then Simran tells Sam that Raj stops the car so Sam asks Simran shall I start Simran feels so shy but doesn't show it. she tells No! Stop. And she gets down from the car. Raj doesn't look at her nor does he says bye! And car just goes away. Simran tells Sam she just stands there and pinch herself she just can't imagine it to be real! Sam was so real that day really Simran loved that even Sam felt that way and tells Simran not to go away. But later on Sam sends an e-mail that she is busy so puts off the chat. Simran was so overwhelmed with the chat that day that she just wanted to feel what she had just talked. She was eager to step in a dream with her friend.

Chat 10: Perhaps the last chat and yes it is! Next day Simran got up with a happy mood. She was forced to pass a very harsh message to Raj and was afraid to think now Raj will get very angry but she couldn't help it the topic was such. But she didn't know Sam will be upset too. Sam comes on a chat with a fighting mood. First only she tells Simran don't talk to me I am in a very bad mood. Simran wonders what has happened to her. She tries to talk very politely to her to change her mood. She again tells Sam to act like Raj may be she will feel better. But Sam says No! Then Simran feels may be she spoke to her yesterday in that way and told her to act like Raj and talk like lover she felt bad but Sam says No! That is not the reason. Now really Simran didn't know what to say. She really feels Sam is Raj and mad on her for her message which she had sent him early in the morning. But then Simran doesn't want to think like that.. she didn't want to think wrong about Raj. Sam continues to fight with her and then she starts giving her names. Now Simran feels very bad she loses all the control and fights back with her. Sam knew very well Simran doesn't like if she gives her name so whenever she wants to make Simran angry she does like that she call her names. Both the friends actually fought that day. Sam tells her she won't come now for Chat. Simran kept asking her what happened why her mood is so off? But Sam doesn't reply she keeps fighting and tells Simran she needs to go. Simran requests her not to go but Sam goes offline and Simran just waits there blank!

Next day Simran sends a message to Sam and asks her if she felt bad when she said to act like Raj but Sam clarifies to her that is not the reason and tells her to find out then she will talk to her. Simran replies if she won't tell her how she is going to find out? Simran is worried now she never thought Sam will get so angry on her. Sam just goes away and yes she can recall now that was the Friday only when they had last spoken!

That day she missed Sam very much so she decides to activate her facebook account. First thing what she always checks whether Raj's name is there in the friends list or not. She finds it missing . . She burst crying don't know why? whenever she sees its not there she feels as if something will happen to her. Then she checks Raj's page and is shocked to see everything was changed there. Once that page belongs to her she thought now it gave completely a stranger look. Raj had included her family and friends photographs on the front page she felt as if all of them are laughing at her. She couldn't take it for long so she just runs away from there. She didn't know what to do she cries and cries. She was not in a proper state of mind. She had everything in life but she only craved for this friendship to happen it meant to her most. Simran thinks how can it be a coincidence that immediately after Sam left her the very next day why all these changes in Raj's pages too? Her heart tells her again and again Sam is only Raj. She decides to deactivate her facebook accounts once more but not before Raj's name is added to the list. Simran once again sends an e-mail to Sam pleading to add Raj's name in the list. But Sam doesn't!

so Simran takes the help of her family he tells her to add his name in the friends list so Raj's page will be added to the list. She tells him to do that and yes Raj's name is added to the list. Simran had kept her facebook account exclusively for Sam her only friend! First time she adds family to restore Raj's name. It was that simple Simran thinks then she recalls why Sam had that evening made her cry and exhausted for more than an hour saying it can't be done? What can be the reason? She thinks! Simran deactivates her account but whenever she does that she feels she is going away from someone who is her own. She feels lost . .

Simran sends her so many messages but Sam doesn't reply. She feels very strongly now that Sam is only Raj and decided not to talk to her. Now that becomes a routine in Simran's life to send message to Sam telling her Sorry. She forgets the count how many messages she sent. In addition to that wait endlessly for her friend to come on chat. Simran simply cries and cries she never cried so much in her life. Now she is most of the time in front of the computer with a hope of her friend to come back. One day Sam sends her the message that she is fed up of her sorrys and has already forgiven her. She specifically tells Simran to leave her life. Simran is shattered . . She feels very bad what she had thought that Sam will come back after one or two days as usual but she never thought Sam will talk to her in such a manner and go away. Now Simran feels so low! Something was breaking inside her heart! It had broken and she could actually feel it.

Simran tries to divert her attention. She gives time for her study and work. But whatever she does the memories of past starts following her and she finds it difficult to concentrate. She tries to be more friendly to Raj but Raj too has changed. She feels that careless attitude of his but doesn't mind because she had only one friend and she didn't want to lose him. She tries to be more extrovert but again here she was mistaken. Raj had so many of that types he craved for her because she was so simple and introvert. She finds Raj's whole attitude is changed. It hurts her she never thought Raj to change like that. She cries like anything whenever she think of going away from Raj. Simran thinks him to be ok after some time. Not directly but indirectly Raj too intentionally says things which hurts her. All this is taking toll on Simran's health. She becomes more weak. She doesn't feel like eating anything when food is served she just look at it. She no more takes care of her. She feels she is just living. But contrast to this she tries to present a different picture about her when she is online or when she is passing messages. Just to show Raj she is normal. But with Sam she still shares everything but never gets reply. Sometimes she feels humiliated but then if she doesn't do that she finds it difficult to survive! Also she had this belief in her mind that one day her friend will return to her. She just can't figure out the exact reason for her friend to get so much angry on her. Again she feels Sam is only Raj and is mad on her for her extreme messages. She prays everyday for her friend to come back and her life once again to fill with joy of friendship. She remembers in the very beginning Sam had told her specifically that it is easy to do a friendship but it is hard to hold that friendship. Simran wishes Sam remembered that.

Chat: Once Simran tries to chat with one of her other friend on her Id who had just gone abroad. As she starts talking to her she remembers Sam and thinks she is talking to Raj. And she feels so heavy she tells her other friend about Sam and that how much she is missing her. That friend tries to make her understand that everything will be all right soon. But Simran couldn't take it longer she just feel like crying. So she tells that friend of hers that they will talk with messages and she can't chat with her and as soon as Simran tells this the power goes off. Simran gets the time to cry and she cries and cries continuously in that darkness she couldn't stop that day . . She decides to block that other friend and also decides never she will chat with anyone else other than Sam. She remembers in the very first chat how much Sam was surprised to know that she never talked to anyone on chat and Sam is the only one she is talking to. Sam didn't believe that so asked her again never? And she had replied never!

Meeting: Simran finally decides to meet Raj to find out if he is her friend. Raj lived in another town very far but Simran had decided to meet him so she does all the preparations for going first time she was going alone. She was so happy in her heart to meet someone who has completely changed her life. For some time she forgets everything. All her pain goes away only to think she is meeting Raj. She informs Raj of her visit and tells him she wants to share something very important so Raj agrees to give her time. Simran is so excited to meet him she does air booking buys a new dress especially for this visit, buys a new laptop just to get one message from Raj if he replies, does the hotel booking and does all the pampering for herself to look presentable! All these only to get one glimpse of her friend. And the day comes when she is all set to meet Raj she informs her family and they don't mind because they knew very well what she was going through. She wanted to look her best she gets ready to meet her friend. And after a long time she feels peace and just didn't want to come out of that. The time is set she gets a message from Raj and is happy to meet. Her heart beats so fast as she is on the way she reaches her destination. She had to wait for sometime but then she didn't mind where he knew she has waited days for this moment. Then she was called she looked at Raj her heart jumps she could actually feel it but controls herself. Both talks very formal with each other Simran just can't believe Raj is in front of her she gives him the gift she brought. She couldn't speak much she only replied to what Raj asked her. She was searching the right words to ask Raj if he is her friend she spoke to! But she couldn't. She takes a leave and again thinks may be Raj was angry when she didn't share anything important or he is still upset with her she didn't know? She is so sad! and comes back with a heavy heart.

Life is again a routine for her. She continues to pass messages to Raj. Somehow she could never come out from her friendship the more she tries the more she falls in that. For her that much is enough that she is honest to her friendship. She sends Sam a message telling her about meeting Raj. She presents a very lovely picture of her meeting. And to her surprise she gets a message from Sam that she is very happy for her and she will talk to her. Simran again thinks Raj has sent that message and she is so happy to again connect to him. She waits for Sam impatiently! But Sam doesn't come. Meanwhile Simran had to prepare for her exams she tries to concentrate on her studies but she can't. The thought of her friend surrounds her. Anyhow she managed to give the exam and pass also. She tries to do something else too. Like working for the NGO driving and helping those in need. But she doesn't feel peace anywhere. Most of the time she is in front of the computer this is where she gets peace. Simran is changed . . Completely changed! She doesn't believe it to be her. She never behaved in that way. First time in her life she felt to put on bet everything she had for her friendship. So much so she loved her friend that she talked most of the time about her friendship.

Life goes like that for Simran each moment is worth only if it is spent in remembering her friend. She gets one more message from Sam saying she is busy with her school and till she get holidays they can talk via messages. Simran is hopeful again and waits . . She does everything with a hope of her friend to come back. She even keeps fast and sacrifices something she likes and so sure she was when she kept fast her friend to come back. She had never kept fast for anyone this is the first time that she felt like doing everything for her friendship. And her fast paid her too. When she visited next to her facebook page she is so happy to see that Raj's page is again like before. Raj had removed those photographs. She feels peace once again. Don't know why but she had become very possessive of her friendship. May be this was because she loved her friend more than herself. She continues to pass messages to Raj even if she thinks they have lost the meaning or don't hold the same value for Raj she is not sure! She doesn't know what will happen to her. She is sinking . . She knows she may fall deep down in the ocean of despair. She is trying in vain to hold herself. She shows she is very strong to Raj but deep inside she is breaking. She pleads her friend not to turn away from her. She loved her friend more than her Life. If she ever spoke to Raj she wants to tell him she loved him the **most**.

Printed in the United States
By Bookmasters